HOW
AGENT PROVOCATEURS
HARM
OUR MOVEMENTS

ICNC
PRESS

How Agent Provocateurs
Harm Our Movements
by Steve Chase
2021

Published by ICNC Press

Publication Disclaimer: The designations
used and material presented in this publication
do not indicate the expression of any opinion
whatsoever on the part of ICNC.

The author holds responsibility for the selection
and presentation of facts contained in this work, as
well as for any and all opinions expressed therein,
which are not necessarily those of ICNC and do
not commit the organization in any way.

This publication was funded in part by
a grant from Humanity United (HU). The opinions
expressed are those of the author and do
not necessarily reflect the views of HU.

International Center on Nonviolent Conflict

600 New Hampshire Ave NW, Suite 710
Washington, D.C. 20037 USA
www.nonviolent-conflict.org

Contact: icnc@nonviolent-conflict.org

HOW
AGENT PROVOCATEURS
HARM
OUR MOVEMENTS

SOME HISTORICAL EXAMPLES
AND A FEW IDEAS
ON REDUCING THE RISK

Steve Chase

CONTENTS

As governments around the world, including our own, face more and more popular resistance, we are witnessing a revival of the use of agent provocateurs.

Bill Heid, "How to Identify an Agent Provocateur"

INTRODUCTION

IN 2011, A YOUNG US JOURNALIST named Chris Steele asked to interview Noam Chomsky, the world-renowned activist scholar. The interview took Steele a couple months to arrange, but eventually he was sitting in Chomsky's faculty office at the Massachusetts Institute of Technology in Cambridge, Massachusetts. Unlike most journalists who talked to Chomsky, Steele started the interview with a question about the impact of agent provocateurs on grassroots movements for human rights, social justice, political freedom, and ecological sustainability (Steele 2012).

Steele originally became interested in the problem of agent provocateurs—fake activists working undercover on behalf of movement opponents—after witnessing their likely presence at an Occupy Wall Street protest he was covering in Denver, Colorado, on October 14, 2011.[1] A frequent visitor to the growing nonviolent encampment of movement supporters, Steele noticed how on that particular day a small group of protesters "who had never been seen before" started rallying other protesters and separating them from the main crowd. These same "protesters" then started engaging in and inciting "vandalism and violence." In the resulting mayhem and confusion, the police

---

1 Note: Some activists and scholars spell the plural term as *agents provocateurs,* which is a direct derivation of the original French term. Others use an anglicized version of the French term and refer to *agent provocateurs*. This article uses the anglicized version throughout, except when directly quoting someone who uses the French-derived spelling.

Photo: Occupy Wall Street demonstration

moved in, attacking the entire encampment, knocking down tents, beating protesters, making arrests, and ultimately evicting all the activists from the public square by force.

In his attempt to understand what he saw that day, Steele interviewed some local Occupy organizers about it. They told him that "these types of actions are typically seen in protests where agent provocateurs have embedded themselves to instigate violence as a means to discredit a nonviolent movement." Intrigued, Steele went to the library and started reading all the literature he could find on "protest and agent provocateurs." This led him to ask Chomsky for an interview.

Steele was still surprised, though, when Chomsky told him that the use of agent provocateurs to repress social movements was "pretty routine" throughout history and in many countries around the world. Speaking of his own early activist experience in the anti-war movement against US military aggression toward Vietnam, Chomsky explained:

> One lesson that we had to learn pretty quickly is that if there is somebody in the group... who's shouting, you know, "Off the cops" or "let's break some windows" or whatever, you're very likely to see him in court testifying for the police, because that's their job, you know, to try to turn activism into something that'll alienate the public... and give them grounds for repression (quoted in Steele 2012).

Chomsky even described the basic pattern of long-term entrapment operations conducted by agent provocateurs that he had learned about "by looking at the FBI cases." Typically, an agent provocateur joins a movement group and then "gets in contact with a bunch of guys" in the group who are at "kind of loose ends." The provocateur looks for vulnerable activists who "don't know what they're doing" or are "confused." The goal here is that when the provocateur "suggests something to them or offers them some money, soon they're trying to stuff a fake bomb somewhere and you arrest them and send them off to jail" (quoted in Steele 2012).

THE USE OF AGENT PROVOCATEURS TO REPRESS SOCIAL MOVEMENTS WAS "PRETTY ROUTINE" THROUGHOUT HISTORY.

Chomsky concluded his answer to Steele by saying, "But that's so routine there's not even any point giving examples" (quoted in Steele 2012). As a long-time activist, I think Chomsky is only half right here. Routine, yes; but the problem of agent provocateurs is still not very well-known by many activists and organizers. Given that this lack of awareness increases a movement's vulnerability to agent provocateurs, I want to share some historical examples of agent provocateur activity around the world, including an in-depth case study from the Black Liberation Movement in the United States. My hope is that this examination will encourage civil resistance organizers to think more deeply about what can be done to minimize the negative impact of agent provocateurs and agent provoca-teur-like behavior on movements for peace, justice, human rights, and sustainability. I then close the essay by sharing some useful first steps toward achieving this goal.

"I am like Hitler... I execute first and give trials afterwards."

General Jorge Ubico Castañeda

Gral. Jorge Ubico

SNAPSHOTS OF AGENT PROVOCATEURS AROUND THE WORLD

I AM CERTAINLY NOT THE FIRST civil resistance activist or scholar to focus on this issue. In the now classic book, *Waging Nonviolent Struggle,* Gene Sharp explains the strategic logic that guides power elites around the world whenever civil resistance movements begin to mobilize. As he notes, power elites routinely seek to weaken these movements by breaking "the resisters' nonviolent discipline" and provoking movement violence through a combination of "severe repression" and employing "spies and *agents provocateurs*" in order to justify more intensive government repression and to damage the movement in the eyes of the public (Sharp 2005).

One illustrative example cited in Sharp's book was during the emergence of the popular nonviolent resistance movement against the dictator of Guatemala in June 1944. Just a month before this Guatemala campaign, the people of El Salvador had successfully used mass civil resistance to end the dictatorial rule of General Maximiliano Hernández Martínez. This victory inspired the people of neighboring Guatemala and panicked General Jorge Ubico Castañeda, who had ruled the country for 13 years. Ubico was a ruthless dictator. In 1934, he had said, "I am like Hitler.... I execute first and give trials afterwards" (quoted in Sharp 2005). In a 1944 public statement, he also said, "As long as I am president, I will never permit a free press, nor free association, because the people of Guatemala are not ready for democracy and need a strong hand" (quoted in Sharp 2005).

Photo: General Jorge Ubico Castañeda, 1926, whose dictatorial rule of Guatemala lasted 13 years until a protest movement caused him to step down

The Guatemala resistance campaign started with very specific and limited reform efforts. The first was a petition by several brave lawyers asking for a corrupt judge to be removed. Then, over 200 National University teachers submitted a petition to the government demanding a wage increase. Soon, students began organizing much larger and more confrontational demonstrations on campus in support of the petition and demanding reinstatement of two fired faculty members, the release of several imprisoned students, and full autonomy and academic freedom at the university. The students also threatened to start a student strike if their demands were not met. When Ubico's government cracked down with martial law, the students began their strike but also mobilized demonstrations off campus and encouraged the Guatemalan people to support them.

After a disciplined student-led march passed the National Palace and the US Embassy one afternoon, a much larger nonviolent demonstration was organized that evening where teachers, lawyers, and some workers joined the students to demand, for the first time, Ubico's resignation. Alarmed by the emerging civil resistance movement against his authoritarian rule, Ubico's government then deployed agent provocateurs to join the ongoing protests and promote property destruction and violence. This led to the police attacking and arresting hundreds of nonviolent protesters, while ignoring the provocateurs.

Luckily, the agent provocateurs were exposed, and people became even more furious with the government. Interestingly, instead of calling for mass demonstrations at the National Palace to protest the government—which organizers feared could be undermined by more skillful agent provocateurs—the movement called for a general strike until Ubico resigned. This shift of tactics proved successful. As Sharp (2005) noted:

> The streets were empty. Workers, businessmen, shopkeepers, market vendors, and bus drivers joined the already striking students, teachers, and lawyers.... The army and police did not know

what to do. Everyone was at home, and there was no target or organized group for them to attack.

The people's victory came remarkably soon after this. On July 1, 1944, General Ubico handed in his letter of resignation and left the Palace. Civil resistance and negotiations continued for a time, followed by elections and a ten-year "springtime of democracy."

Another example of the use of agent provocateurs cited in Sharp's book is from Thailand. On February 23, 1991, a military group calling itself the National Peace Keeping Council (NPKC) launched a coup. A pro-democracy movement emerged in response, gaining strength over time through numerous mass demonstrations, hunger strikes, public criticism of the military regime, and organizing a popular public dialogue process that drafted an alternative "people's constitution" to challenge the military. The movement overwhelmingly adopted disciplined civil resistance as its strategic approach, which put the military rulers at a serious disadvantage. As the main coordinating organization of the movement announced, "our principle was to struggle in a nonviolent way against General Suchinda's appointment [as prime minister] using symbolic and direct action" (quoted in Sharp 2005). A Thai newspaper that remained open also published a translation of a Gene Sharp article on defeating coups through nonviolent resistance, and thousands of leaflets were distributed at mass demonstrations based on Sharp's list of "198 Methods of Nonviolent Action," but were described in Thai as "198 Ways to Fight the Demon."

Unnerved, the military regime released a public warning "that peace and order would be maintained through whatever means necessary" (quoted in Sharp 2005) They increased their repression efforts, but when this did not sufficiently break the discipline of movement participants, the regime started using agent provocateurs to bait activists into using violence against the military government.

Movement leaders suspected this power elite tactic was used when a mass march was blocked on a narrow road by fire engines, a barricade, and a large number of police who started beating people. People were outraged by the beatings and some marchers, though still unarmed, began throwing bricks and bottles at the police and engaging in vandalism. A police station close by was also burned down and the authorities did nothing to stop it. Movement speculation about the number of agent provocateurs involved was intense afterward, since journalists reported the first people damaging nearby vehicles were plain clothed police officers. In subsequent interviews, even two police officers speculated that those who burned the police station were likely agent provocateurs.

Soon after this ragged demonstration, the military government used the supposed movement violence and property destruction as an excuse to declare a state of emergency and then intensified its repression of the pro-democracy movement, including firing into crowds of demonstrators. The largely nonviolent resistance movement ultimately achieved its goal of ending the coup, but casualties were high. At least 52 civilians were killed and at least 300 civilians were injured by gunshots, while approximately 250 people also went missing.

Some movements take the bait in an even bigger way and do not recover or win. The pro-democracy movement in Syria in 2011 is a painful example. When nonviolent protests were at their peak between March and June 2011, caches of weapons were reportedly left by the Assad regime on the streets of rebellious towns (Kahf and Bartkowski 2013), which sidetracked some movement activists into armed struggle. Syria quickly descended into a civil war, and the Assad regime survives to this day.

Other movements, however, have found ways to resist such provocations. For example, some leaders of the movement in Sudan that overthrew dictator Omar al-Bashir in 2019 discovered that agent provocateurs parked vans with arms and ammunition near the sites of mass demonstrations with their doors wide open. Upon discovery of the vans, groups of older women organizers quickly surrounded them to keep

*THE MILITARY GOVERNMENT
USED THE SUPPOSED MOVEMENT
VIOLENCE AS AN EXCUSE TO
DECLARE A STATE OF EMERGENCY
AND THEN INTENSIFIED ITS
REPRESSION.*

young demonstrators from taking the arms into volatile mass demon-strations. In this way, the movement organizers figured out an effective way to inoculate themselves against the negative influences of agent provocateurs and maintain a more effective nonviolent resistance.

Another good example is the independent Polish Solidarity labor movement in the 1980s against the authoritarian Communist regime in Poland led by General Jaruzelski. Through remarkable and tireless popular organizing, the independent trade union developed a mem-bership of 10 million workers and earned widespread public support for the civil resistance actions it led, first for independent unionism, and ultimately for democratic reform of the Soviet-dominated govern-ment. General Jaruzelski responded to this pro-democracy movement with martial law and repression. To increase its advantage, the gov-ernment also embedded many agent provocateurs within Solidarity to urge its members to respond to martial law by organizing a violent overthrow of the Communist government.

As one Solidarity leader reported, the movement resolutely rejected this dangerous and fruitless strategic advice coming in the disguise of supposed union members. They saw it as "the last act of a dying regime" (quoted in York 2000). The advice of provocateurs was simply rejected as a reckless and unstrategic course of action that would have only provided the Soviet Union a justification for invading and occupying Poland. The Solidarity movement's disciplined civil resistance strategy, however, allowed them to end martial law and ultimately bring down the authoritarian government.

Another proven case of an authoritarian regime attempting to use an agent provocateur to no avail was when China sent a former Chinese soldier to Dharamsala, India (the seat of the Tibetan government-in-exile), to "join" the Free Tibet movement. When he was later charged and prosecuted in an Indian court, he testified that he was sent on his mission to nullify charges against him for poor conduct in the Chinese armed services. As a *Tibetan Review* article (2009) noted, "Lei Xun's mission was reported to be to collect, fabricate or otherwise act as an agent provocateur" to validate the Chinese government's claim that the Dalai Lama directly supported rioting and isolated acts of violence that took place during the March 2008 Tibetan uprising. The Chinese agent was rebuffed many times by all his targets in India, who virtually scolded him that the Dalai Lama only supports nonviolent activism. The group's firm commitment to nonviolent conduct in their organizing inoculated the group from the agent provocateur's disruptive tactics.

There are also many examples of the use of agent provocateurs in more democratic countries. For example, following the imposition of draconian laws in India by Prime Minister Indira Gandhi in the mid-to-late 1970s, Sikhs in Punjab began agitating for more state independence from the national government. It has now been documented that in 1984 undercover agent provocateurs working on behalf of the Indian central government began promoting the tactic of an armed occupation of the "Akal Takhat ('Throne of the Immortal') building inside the Golden Temple complex in Amritsar" (Singh 2016). This covert strategy provided India with an excuse to justify a brutal military intervention by the national army and a massive increase in repressive violence throughout much of the Punjab state. Indeed, thousands of Sikhs—now portrayed by the Indian government and the mainstream Indian media as tantamount to bloodthirsty savages—were killed by the Indian army.

A poster showing the face of undercover police officer Mark Kennedy, a.k.a. Mark Stone, was attached to railings at a solidarity picket prior to a hearing into the use of undercover police officers in the infiltration of environmental and social justice campaigns, January 15, 2016.

Another major example is how in 2010 covert police provocateur Mark Kennedy was exposed in the United Kingdom for promoting violence, property destruction, internal discord, and the "radical" demonization of nonviolent activists as sell-outs and fools while posing as an eco-activist and peace activist for seven years using the *nom de guerre* Mark Stone. What triggered his exposure was that "Stone" was arrested in 2009 along with five real activists and charged with conspiring to sabotage a power station. The case collapsed when the other five did some investigation into "Mark Stone's" role and then gave testimony suggesting that Kennedy was an agent provocateur and had not only been the key planner, but had funded the small group's activities, which is illegal under British common law (Lewis and Evans 2011). Activists from at least three other peace or environmental campaigns in Ireland and England also testified that Kennedy infiltrated

THESE TWO "ACTIVISTS" THEN HURRIED TO THE POLICE LINES, SHOWED SOME SORT OF IDS, AND WERE QUICKLY LET THROUGH THE LINES TO DISAPPEAR.

their campaigns, including the Shannonwatch campaign opposing the use of Irish airports by the US military, and Shell to Sea, opposing the Shell Corrib gas project in Mayo, as well as a campaign resisting climate chaos (Belfast Telegraph 2017). One journalist then documented that the police paid Kennedy and funded his operation with tax dollars "up to £250,000 a year" for his efforts to make movements smaller, weaker, and easier to repress (Dodd 2011).

The Mark Kennedy scandal subsequently sparked more sleuthing by journalists from *The Guardian* newspaper in partnership with activists in the UK and across the globe. This partnership group soon set up the Undercover Research Project website. This website has now exposed close to 1,000 cases of proven or likely undercover agent infiltration into social movements in England, Canada, and the European Union. A typical case involves credible witnesses, police denial, and no formal court finding. This was true of the G20 protests in London in 2009. These mass protests were largely nonviolent and those who were tossing stones, breaking windows, burning cars—and urging others to do so—were believed by organizers to be paid agent provocateurs. This suspicion was made more plausible when a participating minister of parliament, Tom Brake, observed two of those activists who were provoking the rest of the crowd suddenly get accused of being police agents by the activists around them. These two "activists" then hurried to the police lines, showed some sort of IDs, and were quickly let through the lines to disappear from the demonstration (Doward and Townsend 2009).

Similarly, in preparation for the 2010 G20 summit in Canada, the Royal Canadian Mounted Police started an 18-month operation involving approximately 500 agents, many of them covert—including some who impersonated global justice activists and even moved in to live with them. Some of these undercover agents attempted to convince global justice activists to commit acts of violence. One journalist wrote about this case, saying:

> Undercover officer Bindo Showan (known during his infiltration as Khalid Mohammed) was asked to stop attending the meetings of an activist group in Guelph because he was pushing an agenda of property damage and violence. Although Showan's identity as a police infiltrator wasn't confirmed until the Crown prosecutor requested in November 2011 that the publication ban regarding the undercover officers be lifted, activists in Southern Ontario had started to suspect him early as 2009. Showan stood out because his actions and suggestions often ran counter to the [nonviolent]style of the groups he was trying to infiltrate (Flegg 2012).

Andre Marin, the Ontario Ombudsman, called the large undercover operation "the most massive compromise of civil liberties in Canadian history" (quoted in Flegg 2012).

Perhaps the biggest public exposure of government surveillance, infiltration, and agent provocateur activity against social movements anywhere in the world occurred in the United States following a late-night activist break-in of the Federal Bureau of Investigation's local office in Media, Pennsylvania, in 1971. As noted in the documentary film *1971,* this small group of peace activists was fed-up by ongoing repression against free speech, the right to assemble, and seeking a redress of grievances from a supposedly democratic government (Hamilton 2014). What these activists found, after studying their many boxes of stolen documents, was clear confirmation of the existence and activities of the FBI's now-infamous campaign

Redacted COINTELPRO FBI Memo, 1970

against peace and social justice movements. They then made sure
this information got to major news organizations and sympathetic
members of the US Congress, who started public hearings.

The documents, hearings, and investigative reporting revealed
disturbing evidence. Between 1956 and 1971, the FBI, in coordination

with local police departments, ran what it called counterintelligence programs (*COINTELPRO* for short) against numerous social movements seeking peace and justice reforms through a combination of normal institutional channels and civil resistance tactics, as well as a few groups arguing for armed self-defense. As Ward Churchill and Jim Vander Wall (1990) quote from their massive published collection of these documents, *The COINTELPRO Papers*, the stated goals of these operations were to "disrupt and destabilize," "cripple," "destroy," and "neutralize" popular movements seeking social justice, equality, human rights, and peace. The government's COINTELPRO campaign on behalf of US power elites were even described by a congressional investigator as "a sophisticated vigilante operation" (quoted in Churchill and Vander Wall 1990).

Churchill and Vander Wall also identify several core elements of COINTELPRO operations, one of which was the extensive use of agent provocateurs embedded within progressive social movements. These documents revealed, for example, the use of agent provocateurs in the peace movement opposing the US war against the Vietnamese people. Targeted groups included Students for a Democratic Society (SDS), Vietnam Veterans Against the War (VVAW), and the National Mobilization Committee to End the War in Vietnam.

Gary Marx, a sociologist researching US agent provocateurs, also reports several similar examples in his work. One of the most revealing is about the FBI provocateur nicknamed "Tommy the Traveler." Citing stories in *The New York Times,* Marx (1974) explains:

> *"Tommy the Traveler," posing as an SDS organizer, offered bombs, guns, and lessons in guerilla tactics to students on various New York campuses. Two students whom he had taught to make Molotov cocktails burned down the campus ROTC building and were immediately arrested.*

Even more telling, Tommy the Traveler admitted, "There's a thousand guys in the field like me" (quoted in Marx 1974).

AGENT PROVOCATEURS WORKING TO WEAKEN THE US BLACK LIBERATION MOVEMENT

ONE OF THE MOST SHOCKING revelations about the COINTELPRO program was that it heavily targeted the nonviolent movement seeking justice and human rights for African Americans in the 1950s and 1960s. The FBI particularly focused on Martin Luther King, Jr., and his Southern Christian Leadership Conference (SCLC) organization, which helped organize civil resistance campaigns for voting and other human rights for Black citizens from 1957 onward. Yet, the FBI's surveillance of King and the SCLC was just an escalation of their longstanding investigation of the National Association for the Advancement of Colored People (NAACP), which began well before the FBI started officially using the term COINTELPRO to describe its covert, repressive, anti-movement operations.

The NAACP had restricted itself to normal institutional tactics of policy change such as lawsuits and lobbying, but because of their goal of racial justice, which did not serve power elite interests at the time, their leadership and most active members were watched, wire-tapped, and informed on by FBI infiltrators. The official justification for this in FBI public statements was to search for "communist dominance" in the organization and prove that the organization was under the influence of a "hostile foreign power" (quoted in Churchill and Vander Wall 1990).

Photo: Martin Luther King Jr. arrested in Montgomery, Alabama

However, no such evidence was ever found, even after extensive investigation from 1941 until 1966 involving 151 informants, close to 3,000 illegal wiretaps, and over 800 bugs placed in the homes of members and the meeting rooms of the organization. Even so, the FBI tried to force all the members of the NAACP to register with the government as subversives until this abuse of the US Constitution was blocked by the US Supreme Court.

King's SCLC was considered even more dangerous to power elite interests than the NAACP because it was mobilizing many thousands, and ultimately millions, of Black Americans and their allies to engage in mass civil resistance campaigns for human rights and social justice—and these nonviolent resistance campaigns were increasingly winning real reforms. The panic only grew as King started linking the issues of racism, militarism, and economic inequality and called for even bigger structural changes in US society. King's last organizing effort before his assassination in 1968 was the Poor People's Campaign. This campaign, initiated by the SCLC, was working to build a national interracial coalition using militant civil resistance tactics in support of a broad economic justice agenda that King hoped would start a shift in the United States to a more democratic political and economic alternative to both corporate capitalism and communism.

What is now known about the FBI's once-secret attempt to destroy the social justice movements associated with King is instructive. It began with a 1957 memo from the national headquarters of the FBI to its office in Atlanta, Georgia, after King had led the successful Montgomery Bus Boycott in 1955-56. The memo included a press clipping about the founding of SCLC and ordered the local office to start surveillance of the SCLC's staff office, stating, "in view of the stated purpose of the organization you should remain alert for public source information concerning it in connection with the racial situation" (quoted in Churchill and Vander Wall 1990).

By 1960, the FBI began extensive infiltration of the organization, and by 1963, Robert F. Kennedy, the US Attorney General, had authorized phone taps of all SCLC's regional offices and King's residence and motel rooms, as well as office break-ins of King's associates. As noted by Churchill and Vander Wall (1990):

The reasons for this covert but steadily mounting attention to the Reverend Dr. King were posited in an internal monograph on the subject prepared by FBI counter-intelligence specialist Charles D. Brennan at the behest of COINTELPRO head William C. Sullivan in September 1963. In this 11-page document, Brennan found that, given the scope of support it had attracted over the preceding five years, civil rights agitation represented a clear threat to "the established order" of the U.S., and that "King is growing in stature daily as the leader among leaders of the Negro movement... so goes Martin Luther King, and also so goes the Negro movement in the United States."

William Sullivan also wrote a memo after the massive 1963 March on Washington for Jobs and Freedom that featured King's famous "I Have a Dream" speech. In it, Sullivan shared the FBI leadership's view that, "We must mark him now, if we have not before, as the most dangerous Negro in the future of the nation" (quoted in Churchill and Vander Wall 1990). He even called King a threat to "national security." He added ominously, "it may be unrealistic to limit [our actions against King] to legalistic proofs that would stand up in court or before Congressional Committees" (quoted in Churchill and Vander Wall 1990).

This meant planting negative stories about King in compliant news outlets. When that didn't do the job of destroying King's leadership, and King was even named the winner of the 1964 Nobel Peace Prize, Sullivan authorized a more chilling COINTELPRO operation. Sullivan instructed his agents to edit the FBI audio tapes of King's sexual infidelities in motel rooms across the country and send it to King with an anonymous letter telling him to commit suicide before receiving the prize or the tapes would be released publicly. The agents did this, but it didn't work. King didn't buckle under this blackmail.

With growing frustration, the FBI leadership soon expanded its program of planting agent provocateurs within the human rights and social justice campaigns associated with King in order to create divisions, rivalries, scandals, and a decline in nonviolent discipline. As one FBI memo instructed its undercover agents and assets embedded within various movement campaigns, they were now authorized to "inspire action in instances where circumstances warrant" (quoted in Churchill and Vander Wall 1990). This marked a fully authorized and widespread shift from agents working primarily as undercover informants to becoming active agent provocateurs.

From the mid-1960s on, federal and local police vastly expanded their disruption of social movement organizations and coalitions through agent provocateurs, including King's SCLC, the Student Nonviolent Coordinating Committee (SNCC), the Congress of Racial Equality (CORE), the Poor People's Campaign, and a myriad of ongoing local nonviolent direct action campaigns. By 1967, these various operations were consolidated into what the FBI called "COINTELPRO–Black Liberation Movement," and the number of local FBI offices involved rose from 23 to 41. From 1967 to 1968, the number of agents involved in this COINTELPRO operation rose from 1,246 to 1,678.

For the FBI, the results of their efforts were promising. Exploiting the despair, frustration, and anger of many sincere activists, agent provocateurs were able to weaken movements through inciting factionalism, rivalries, scandals, and fostering a significant decline of nonviolent discipline and a growing drift to various levels of social movement violence. For example, after much acrimonious factionalism, SNCC leaders H. Rap Brown and Stokely Carmichael changed the name of the organization from the Student Nonviolent Coordinating Committee to the Student National Coordinating Committing. Brown and Carmichael also rhetorically embraced violent self-defense at mass demonstrations, and, increasingly over time, even offensive political violence. This only created more room for agent provocateurs to maneuver.

The cultural zeitgeist began to shift and riots in many inner cities emerged, which helped justify even more intense government repression and decreased public support for the racial justice movement. As African American Studies scholar Manning Marable explains:

> *In the spring and summer months of 1964, 1965, 1966, 1967 and 1968, massive black rebellions swept across almost every major US city in the Northeast, Middle West and California.... Combining the total weight of socio-economic destruction, the ghetto rebellions from 1964 to 1972 led to 250 deaths, 10,000 serious injuries, and 60,000 arrests, at a cost of police, troops, and other coercive measures taken by the state and losses to business in the billions of dollars (quoted in Churchill and Vander Wall 1990).*

It is possible that part of this rioting was directly sparked or fanned by agent provocateurs. Yet, the documentary record tends to focus more on the infiltration of agent provocateurs within ongoing, organized social movement efforts.

One group that was explicitly organized as a violent flank within the Black Liberation Movement was the Black Panther Party, founded in Oakland, California, in 1966. It soon had chapters in dozens of cities. At the beginning, the Panthers had three major focuses: local electoral campaigning; direct service programs such as school breakfasts and after-school programs; and armed patrols in the inner city to protect Black people from police brutality and harassment. The FBI immediately targeted the group and used agent provocateurs to promote internal divisions, encourage the Panthers to move into offensive violence, and demonize the group's image in the public mind to justify intense repression, including police assignations of some of its leadership.

Churchill and Vander Wall wrote a whole book entitled *Agents of Repression* on this topic, but other researchers have also documented the FBI's war against the Black Panthers, including the government's use of agent provocateurs. As *New York Times* writer Giovanni Russonello (2016) pointed out:

> *It was not until years later that the Senate's Church Committee would show how pervasively the F.B.I. worked against the Panthers and how much it influenced press coverage. It encouraged urban police forces to confront Black Panthers; planted informants and agent provocateurs; and intimidated local community members who were sympathetic to the group.*

Gary Marx (1974) also offers a summary of some of the activities of FBI and local police used against the Panthers. Here are just a few of his examples—out of many:

- In New York, 13 Black Panthers accused of conspiring to bomb public places reportedly received 60 sticks of dynamite from an FBI informant.

- A New York detective helped open the Harlem office and then helped the Bronx chapter of the Black Panthers. He joined the party before any of those he testified against in the Panther 13 trial. He acknowledged that his activities went beyond mere infiltration.

- Another undercover policeman had charge of the distribution of the Panther newspaper in the metropolitan area and was acting lieutenant of finance.

- In another case involving the Black Panthers in Indiana and New York, police agents reportedly induced Black militants to burglarize and rob a bank, offering them weapons, a map of the target, and even a getaway car.

- The raid in Chicago where Fred Hampton and Mark Clark were killed was based on an FBI informant's report of a weapons cache, though few weapons were found. The chief of security for the Panthers at this time and Hampton's bodyguard was a paid FBI informant. In court testimony, he revealed his duties to be "making sure that all members were properly armed and their weapons working, screening and investigating possible informers and building security devices.

*THE FBI LEADERSHIP SOON
EXPANDED ITS PROGRAM OF
PLANTING AGENT PROVOCATEURS
WITHIN THESE HUMAN RIGHTS
AND SOCIAL JUSTICE CAMPAIGNS.*

Interestingly, while Churchill and Vander Wall remain firm believers in the idea that violent resistance is a more effective and powerful alternative compared to civil resistance, they actually document in great detail how power elites used agent provocateurs to change the character of movements—to make them more violent and thus smaller, less effective, and easier to repress without public backlash. As their work reveals so well, operations like COINTELPRO harm movements and decrease their effectiveness. These two authors even muse that such efforts "perhaps accounts for much of the negativity with which the black liberation movement came to be publicly viewed by the end of the 1960s" (Churchill and Vander Wall 1990).

Research by Princeton University professor Omar Wasow confirms Churchill and Vander Wall's hypothesis that such shifts toward violence by some movement groups led to public perceptions that harmed the movement for racial justice in the United States during the 1960s. Wasow's 2016 working draft article "Do Protests Matter? Evidence from the 1960s Black Insurgency" (which was adapted and published by the *American Political Science Review* in early 2021) looks closely at the different impacts on voting patterns, public opinion, and the discourse of political thought leaders in response to:

1. riots and violent tactics, such as those promoted by agent provocateurs; and, in contrast,

2. disciplined nonviolent tactics, which agent provocateurs seek to undermine.

Through a complex research design that evaluated county-level data and voting patterns, Wasow discovered that proximity to disciplined civil resistance (i.e., nonviolent protests) resulted in white people focusing on the issue of "equality" and "civil rights," while proximity to violent protests and riots shifted their focus to "law and order" and made them more supportive of state repression against the Black Liberation Movement. Nonviolent protests also "helped to grow the egalitarian coalition of white liberals, white moderates, and blacks," but protests perceived as violent strengthened an opposing coalition that pushed a more racist and authoritarian outlook. These shifts had major repercussions on politics and society. Critically, Wasow (2016) found that "in Presidential elections, the proximity to black-led nonviolent protests caused increased white Democratic vote share, whereas proximity to black-led violent protests caused substantially important decline and likely tipped the 1968 election from Hubert Humphrey to Richard Nixon." Wasow (2016) closes with this conclusion: "Tactics matter... and while violence in response to repression is often justifiable, this research suggests it may not be strategic."

Despite agent provocateur activity and agent provocateur-like behavior that harmed and weakened US social movements in the late 1960s, some important reforms were still won. The decline in movement effectiveness was mitigated to an important degree by persistence in disciplined civil resistance strategies by many movement activists and by the public exposure of agent provocateur activity in the early and mid-1970s. The news media and congressional hearings on the undemocratic behavior of the FBI and CIA certainly helped spark some public backlash.

This public exposure also resulted in the FBI and local police departments ending use of the name and language of COINTELPRO and becoming even more secretive about such activities. Indeed, the FBI started engaging in massive public relations efforts to seemingly reject the "bad old" FBI of much of the 20th century and contrast it with the supposedly "new," democratic, and reformed FBI that no longer engaged in such police-state tactics. Instead of talking about political subversives whose focus on peace, justice, and environmental quality made them threats to the "established order of the United States," the terms of art were now about "terrorists" and "violent extremists." With this rhetorical sleight of hand, after the early 1970s, COINTELPRO operations continued under new names targeting nonviolent groups, regardless of whether those groups used normal institutional channels or civil resistance. Agent provocateurs also pushed armed self-defense groups like the American Indian Movement into offensive political violence. Tellingly, Churchill and Vander Wall's book *The COINTELPRO Papers* concludes with a chapter entitled "COINTELPRO Lives On." As they (1990) explain:

> *The results of such linguistic subterfuge were... readily evidenced during the 1980s when it was revealed that the FBI had employed the rubric of a "terrorist investigation" to rationalize the undertaking of a multi-year "probe" of the nonviolent CISPES [Committee In Solidarity with the People of El Salvador] organization—extended to encompass at least 215 other groups, including Clergy and Laity Concerned, the Maryknoll Sisters, Amnesty International, the Chicago Interreligious Task Force, the U.S. Catholic Conference, and the Virginia Education Association—opposed to U.S. policy in Central America. Needless to say, the CISPES operation was attended by systematic resort to such time-honored COINTELPRO tactics as the use of infiltrators/provocateurs, disinformation, "black bag jobs" [ie. clandestine breaking and entry operations,] telephone intercepts, "conspicuous surveillance (to make targets believe 'there's an agent behind every mail box')," and so on.*

More recently, a similar power elite effort to smear movements as violent and destructive was attempted to some effect by then-President Donald Trump as he demonized the Movement for Black Lives uprisings in 2020 that were organized to protest institutional racism

AFTER THE EARLY 1970S, COINTELPRO OPERATIONS CONTINUED UNDER NEW NAMES TARGETING NONVIOLENT GROUPS.

and police brutality after the May 25 police murder of George Floyd in Minneapolis, Minnesota. Trump repeatedly blamed—without offering any evidence—anarchists and movement supporters for the arson, looting, and street violence that accompanied a few of the early protests around the country. He tried to smear this entire civil resistance movement with these marginal activities and called all the protesters "low-lifes" and "thugs," even though a detailed study discussed in *The Washington Post* showed that out of the thousands of Black Lives Matter demonstrations in the United States during 2020, "96.3 involved no property damage or police injuries, and in 97.7 percent of events, no injuries were reported among participants, bystanders, or police" (Chenoweth and Perryman 2020).

Trump's smear tactic was made easier by the distortions of right-wing media and the fact that in August 2017, the FBI issued a report with the title, "Black Identity Extremists Likely Motivated to Target Law Enforcement Officers" (FBI Counterterrorism Division 2017). This official report targeted groups like the Movement for Black Lives, while largely ignoring the unlawful white supremacist militias that FBI leadership later publicly recognized as highly threatening for domestic terrorism. Based on the FBI's past behavior patterns, its 2017 report seemed to open a path to surveillance and possible agent provocateur activity against nonviolent activist groups protesting police violence toward unarmed Black people.

Yet, efforts to smear the movement as violent were not as effective in 2020 as they were in the late 1960s and early 1970s. For one thing, many Movement for Black Lives organizers were very persistent in their mass civil resistance efforts and often disassociated themselves from the people engaged in arson, looting, and street fighting. They also raised the issue of agent provocateurs and false flag operations by armed militia groups like the Boogaloo Bois as a part of the violence and property destruction that happened during the protests. One important example was the widely reported case of how a white supremacist, dubbed "Umbrella Man," pretended to be a Black Lives Matter supporter in Minneapolis and was the first to start indiscriminate property damage at the margins of a multi-racial nonviolent demonstration in order to discredit the BLM movement (Jany 2020).

Some mass media outlets also seemed less complicit than they often were in the 1960s. As media commentator Deborah Mathis (2020) writes:

> Early coverage portrayed the demonstrations as a threat to public peace and security, with rioters and looters enabling the movement's message to be slandered. However, this soon receded, as many activists distanced themselves from these behaviors and shared examples of provocateurs and infiltrators engaging in violent acts. Once rid of this sideshow, cameras captured nonviolent protesters—an overwhelming majority—sitting in parks, kneeling in prayer, or gathering around a group of violinists…. The violence that has occurred has been, primarily, by the hands of law enforcement in its ironically brutish response to people protesting police brutality.

All this helped make government repression backfire and benefit the movement to a significant degree. Yet, we can already see how agent provocateur activities can be used by power elites and movement opponents to weaken the unity of civil resistance movements, discredit them in the eyes of the wider public, and justify greater and more draconian repression by police and security forces.

POURING OIL ON THE FIRE?

UNFORTUNATELY, SOME SINCERE, but misguided, activists unwittingly do the work of agent provocateurs—or end up facilitating greater agent provocateur influence within our movements. Some of these voices make fairly sophisticated arguments and can sound persuasive. I could cite several examples here, but let me pick just one—Ben Case's 2017 article published in *ROAR Magazine*. In his piece, Case echoes many other sincere activists in movements around the world by arguing that combining violent and nonviolent tactics can increase the effectiveness of movements struggling against oppression and injustice.

Along the way, Case makes several good points in his essay. Who can disagree, for example, that we should select tactics "based on the potential of those actions to disrupt oppressive systems, build power, and win short-term goals that can lead to long-term victories." He is right that the most important distinction to be made when selecting tactics is between making strategic tactical choices (that have the highest probability of increasing movement effectiveness) and making unstrategic tactical choices (that might fulfill some activists' romantic fantasies or transient emotional needs, but actually backfire against a movement and lower its probability of success).

He even argues that full-scale armed struggle is not helpful in increasing movement effectiveness and cites the groundbreaking research of Erica Chenoweth and Maria Stephan in their award-winning

Photo: Protesters in black bloc, commonly called "Antifa," march in Montreal

CAMPAIGNS WITH LOWER NONVIOLENT DISCIPLINE SPARKED LESS-POWERFUL BACKFIRE EFFECTS AGAINST THEIR GOVERNMENT'S USE OF REPRESSION.

book *Why Civil Resistance Works*. As Case explains, these two researchers have convincingly demonstrated that predominately "nonviolent movements are twice as likely as violent ones to achieve 'maximalist' political goals (overthrowing a leader, ousting a foreign occupation or seceding from a territory)." He also acknowledges that violent tactics tend to "generate greater police repression" and that "mainstream tolerance for police repression," particularly of violent protests, "is quite high."

Case also suggests that an effective 21st century revolutionary will look more like a Gandhian civil resister than a "Maoist or Guevarist guerrilla." As he notes approvingly, most social change "activists today do not seriously discuss taking up arms and going to the mountains to wage guerrilla warfare." He also praises scholars studying civil resistance for articulating many "user-friendly approaches for dismantling institutional targets using creative nonviolent disruption." As he notes, "Key principles of civil resistance such as noncooperation, mass participation, polarization, and the backfiring effect are important and useful."

However, after making all these solid points, Case then makes a sudden leap of logic and claims out of nowhere that there are "many reasons" to believe that today's movements will be far more effective if they supplement their nonviolent civil resistance tactics with the frequent "use of low-level violent actions," which he describes as rioting, breaking windows, street-fighting with violent police, punching counter-demonstrators, and arson. Unfortunately, he does not offer any evidence to support his assertion. All he offers is the observation that the original Nonviolent and Violent Conflicts and Outcomes (NAVCO) dataset used by leading scholars to draw comparisons between the dynamics and impacts of nonviolent and violent movements is not finely calibrated enough to conclusively rule out his evidence-free assertion about the superior effectiveness of mixing nonviolent tactics with low-level violent actions (which he and others refer to as supporting a "diversity of tactics").

Yet, as I noted earlier, Omar Wasow's (2016) findings on the 1960s US Black insurgency offer strong evidence that working to foster greater nonviolent discipline within our movements is a more strategic approach than the so-called diversity of tactics approach advocated by Case and others. Further research also supports this conclusion. For example, in her book *Nonviolent Revolutions*, Sharon Erickson Nepstad (2011) looks at paired comparative case studies of civil resistance campaigns against Communist regimes, military dictatorships, and personal dictators. In each category, she discovered that the failed national civil resistance movements had significantly lower levels of nonviolent discipline than the three successful cases she examined. Her conclusion is that the campaigns with lower nonviolent discipline sparked less-powerful backfire effects against their government's use of repression and fewer defections among the police, military, and security services than the successful cases she examined.

Erica Chenoweth has also continued to do groundbreaking research on this topic. Chenoweth finds that, since the 2000s, a higher number of civil resistance campaigns have emerged globally than in previous decades. That is the good news. The bad news is that, while civil resistance campaigns are still well over twice as effective as violent campaigns, their overall success rate since 2006 has been declining. Why? In a 2016 policy brief entitled "The Rise of Nonviolent Resistance," Chenoweth raises four likely reasons for this development that deserve consideration. One of the most important is that, since 2006, "a higher proportion of primarily nonviolent uprisings tolerate, embrace, or fail to contain violent flanks" (Chenoweth 2016). Chenoweth then offers a graph that documents an increase in the rates of violent flanks alongside civil resistance campaigns during the very period of decline in the effectiveness of civil resistance campaigns.

Figure 1: The Decline of Nonviolent Discipline During the Post-2006 Decline in Civil Resistance Effectiveness

Source: Erica Chenoweth, "The Rise of Nonviolent Resistance," *PRIO Policy Brief* 19 (2016).

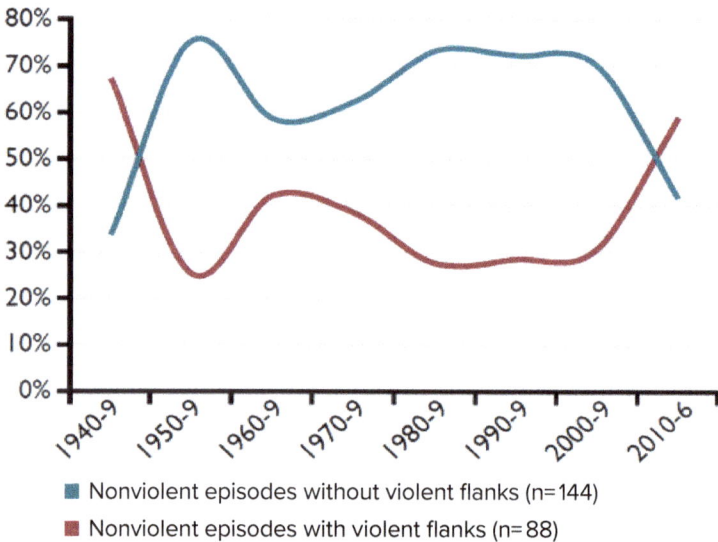

■ Nonviolent episodes without violent flanks (n=144)
■ Nonviolent episodes with violent flanks (n=88)

These findings, and the updated findings in Chenoweth's (2020) article on "The Future of Nonviolent Resistance," suggest that activists and organizers should be very skeptical of the claims made by sincere activists who advocate for or engage in the use of low-level violence or even more destructive violence alongside organized civil resistance activities.

Beyond the research itself, the strongest line of evidence that contradicts the diversity of tactics claims for me is the little discussed, but now well-documented, fact that agent provocateurs have long advocated violent tactics in order to harm otherwise nonviolent movements. Their motives are different from sincere activists, of course. They do not see such behavior as strengthening movements. Indeed, the power elites that hire agent provocateurs clearly understand that undermining a movement's nonviolent discipline and encouraging low-level violence makes movements easier to defeat. If this was not the case, how likely would it be that oppressive regimes all over the world would continue to spend significant time, human resources, and money trying to get activists in social movements to engage in such violent activities?

I find it painfully telling that no agent provocateur has ever been documented encouraging a movement to adopt a disciplined civil resistance strategy and the arguments used by agent provocateurs are often mimicked by sincere, but misguided, activists. The kinds of arguments justifying violence I have repeatedly heard over the years include:

- Only cowards shrink from violence.
- Evil must be smashed by any and all means.
- Violence is far more radical, and when injustice is extreme, a more radical response is required.
- Violence is a faster way to get the change we need.
- We have a right to defend ourselves.
- We face powerful enemies and violence is the power we need.
- It is stupid to limit our options.
- Even if you think that movement violence is usually unstrategic, you have to be inclusive of people who disagree with you, or else you are being intolerant and violating people's freedom to do as they wish.
- Those who are violent motivate the enemy to negotiate with the more moderate ones, our less-brave allies.
- We will give up our violent options only when the government and all our other enemies give up their option to be violent to us.
- Violence is the only language the oppressor understands.
- Our futures have been looted from us. LOOT BACK.

One young activist that I talked to a couple of years back said, "It has surprised me how many people in my social media bubble support Black Bloc/Antifa stuff," especially their calling for a "diversity of tactics." This slogan has indeed proven to be a very effective way to market violence to activists—or at least the tolerance of violence. It sounds strategic and inclusive, right? However, that depends on whether we are talking about a diversity of *effective* tactics that increase movement participation and power over time, or a poorly thought-out hodgepodge of counterproductive violent tactics tacked onto civil resistance actions in ways that often decrease movement participation and effectiveness. While the "diversity of tactics" slogan sounds good, the phrase, which is often used by agent provocateurs, is really just an effective way to sell this second, very defective, pro-violence outlook to unsuspecting activists.

Countering the marketing of ineffective violence will take effort. One activist I talked with told me that she believes that more activists need to speak up and challenge the fuzzy thinking behind the "diversity of tactics" slogan. She talked about being at a conference on social movements where a presenter "was totally pushing for 'diversity of tactics' as his right." She added, "Had I had an opportunity, I would have liked to talk with him and other conference attendees about how the 'right to use violence' is not just an individual choice." She makes a good point. In a dark alley when you are one-on-one with a violent attacker, it might be productive to use counter-violence to save your life. An individual or a small group of activists using such violence at a mass movement action, however, can put many innocent people in danger, often in violation of democratic group agreements, and it does not work well in minimizing the severity of oppression or winning victory against an opponent with overwhelming violent force and material resources. It actually decreases the chances of collective victory.

Claiming an individual right to engage in violence at organized civil resistance actions is like a corporation claiming the right to make harmful

A black bloc protester graffities "Kill all cops" over a public advertisement

production choices regardless of the negative impacts on its workers, customers, or external third parties. This "right" to corporate liberty is seen by some free market fundamentalists as sacred. Many people simply acquiesce to this distorted notion of free enterprise—another positive sounding marketing term—even though they suspect this approach actually corrupts our economy and harms both people and planet.

There is a real parallel here. Some activists who would never engage in counterproductive movement violence themselves routinely get tongue-tied, passive, or confused when a tiny minority of activists invoke the positive sounding rhetoric of a "diversity of tactics" and "individual rights" to use violence. This passivity in the face of the marketing of violence is troublesome because it does not help movements win. It makes success that much harder—and it makes it much easier for actual agent provocateurs to have a stronger negative influence within our movements.

RESPONDING EFFECTIVELY

I STRONGLY BELIEVE THAT developing an awareness of the problem of agent provocateurs and agent provocateur-like behavior can help all activists and organizers become more effective. Yet, this awareness is not sufficient by itself. The next needed step is to explore and experiment with the ways activists and organizers can work together to inoculate our movements against the negative influence of agent provocateur-like behavior, no matter who engages in it.

Not all activist responses in the past have proven effective in addressing this very real problem. As Gary Marx (1974) notes, movement responses to agent provocateurs have typically varied at the extremes from "ignoring them," on the one hand, to "the use of rigid security techniques and paranoid suspicion of everyone," on the other. Neither of these extremes have proven very effective, or if effective in the short-term, the cure itself can also be very damaging to overall movement growth. Offering an example of this counterproductive phenomenon from the 1960s Black Liberation Movement in the United States, Marx notes that the Black Panthers "stopped accepting new members during one period in an effort to avoid infiltration."

In another example, in 2019 pro-democracy protesters occupying the airport in Hong Kong noticed one participant's counter-productive behavior and suspected he was an agent provocateur in their midst. Several demonstrators then "grabbed him, and frisked him and found that the name on his passport [Xu Jinyang] matched that of an auxiliary policeman from the nearby city of Shenzhen" (Sweet 2019). In response, they immediately tied him up and then roughed him up. Soon they were kicking him hard—"a decision that might have led to his death, had it not been for the intervention of a local reporter, Richard Scotford, who shielded the accused man and warned the crowd that his ill treatment would be a propaganda coup for the mainland." It turns out this journalist was right, as footage of these events was used for stories portraying the movement as a violent threat. Because of their impulsive and very counterproductive response to Xu Jinyang, he was actually quite successful in his mission, even though he was caught.

To be more successful in our work, we have to find better ways to address the problem of agent provocateur-like behavior in our movements. Activist Lisha Sterling provides some guidance. She first notes how it can be difficult, and even damaging, to try to tell the difference between agent provocateurs and sincere, but misguided, activists. Sterling (2020) then advises to focus more on the behavior rather than the suspected underlying motivation, stating:

> In the end, there may well be some people whom you never figure out are infiltrators until long after everything is over. The best solution to the problem of the unknown infiltrator is not to distrust everyone, but rather to avoid this potentially disastrous tension altogether by adopting and enforcing a clear code of conduct for all participants. If you isolate people who refuse to maintain your agreed upon security protocols or who break your code of conduct, then you will have effectively defeated the enemy in your camp.

Beyond this, activists should be prepared to argue our case internally for why nonviolent methods are needed and why violence carries high probabilities of backfire against the movement and heightens the risk of movement failure. Whether the marketing of violence comes from an undercover agent provocateur or from a sincere but misguided activist, the most important antidote is to be bold and raise strategic questions and perspectives within movement dialogues and debates, rather than accusing them of bad motives. We need to learn how to

THE BEST SOLUTION IS NOT TO DISTRUST EVERYONE, BUT RATHER TO AVOID THIS POTENTIALLY DISASTROUS TENSION BY ENFORCING A CLEAR CODE OF CONDUCT FOR ALL.

challenge the many unhelpful assumptions behind the "diversity of tactics" slogan and start calling it out for what it is: the marketing of violence that has historically been promoted by agent provocateurs. Other useful actions that can help our movements succeed include:

- Promoting more evidence-based social science research on movement effectiveness in order to undermine unsupported conventional thinking and romantic revolutionary notions with little strategic validity;

- Educating more activists and organizers in effective civil resistance history and strategy, as well as the history and strategy of the power elites' use of agent provocateurs;

- Shifting at times to different civil resistance tactics that may be less vulnerable to agent provocateur incitement and increase the possibility that violent repression against a nonviolent movement will backfire, increase popular participation, and lead to more defections from the targeted institution's pillars of support;

- Stating a clear collective commitment to nonviolent discipline in all our calls for action and avoiding the rhetoric of "diversity of tactics";

- Providing trainings before major resistance actions explaining why maintaining nonviolent discipline increases movement effectiveness.

- Helping people develop the capacity to keep their eyes on the prize in the face of repression and the incitement of agent provocateurs or misguided activists;

- Encouraging the formation of smaller movement affinity/support groups as cells within a larger action to help maintain effective behavior, increase personal accountability, provide mutual aid, and help people deal with their emotions in the face of violent repression and provocation;
- Using trained peacekeepers at our actions to help well-meaning activists not take the bait to engage in impulsive, but unhelpful, movement behavior;
- Challenging macho posturing within our movement culture and encouraging the full participation of women in the leadership of people's movements (which research indicates usually improves nonviolent discipline and movement effectiveness considerably).

There will likely always be agent provocateurs who try to sow division and encourage or use violence, as well as some sincere activists who promote discredited and counterproductive notions about the benefits of movement violence. We just do not have to buy what they are selling or stay silent about the ineffectiveness or destructiveness of their ideas and actions. By developing our capacity to resist the marketing of movement violence, we can make our movements more successful and inoculate ourselves from the harm caused by agent provocateurs and agent provocateur-like behavior. This will ultimately increase our chances of winning victories for rights, freedom, justice, and sustainability.

REFERENCES

"About Us." Undercover Research Project. Accessed October 4, 2021, https://undercoverresearch.net/about-us-2/.

"Activist 'Bitterly Disappointed' by 'Closed' Report into Undercover Policing." *Belfast Telegraph,* February 6, 2017. https://www.belfasttelegraph.co.uk/news/republic-of-ireland/activist-bitterly-dis-appointed-by-closed-report-into-undercover-policing-35427120.html.

FBI Counterterrorism Division. "Black Identity Extremists Likely Motivated to Target Law Enforcement Officers." 2017. *FBI Intelligence Assessment.* https://assets.documentcloud.org/documents/4067711/BIE-Redacted.pdf.

Case, Ben. "Beyond Violence and Nonviolence." *ROAR Magazine* 5 (June 2017). https://roarmag.org/magazine/beyond-violence-nonviolence-antifascism/.

Chenoweth, Erica. "The Rise of Nonviolent Resistance." *PRIO Policy Brief* 19. Oslo: Peace Research Institute Oslo, 2016. https://www.prio.org/Publications/Publication/?x=9202.

Chenoweth, Erica. "The Future of Nonviolent Resistance." *Journal of Democracy* 31, no. 3 (2020): 69–84.

Chenoweth, Erica, and Jerry Pressman. "This Summer's Black Lives Protesters Were Overwhelming Peaceful, Our Research Finds." *The Washington Post,* October 16, 2020.

Chenoweth, Erica, and Maria J. Stephan. *Why Civil Resistance Works: The Strategic Logic of Nonviolent Conflict.* New York: Columbia University Press, 2011.

"Chinese Agent Provocateur Caught in D'sala." *Tibetan Review: The Monthly Magazine on All Aspects of Tibet* 44, no. 2 (2009): 12–13.

Churchill, Ward, and Jim Vander Wall. *The COINTELPRO Papers: Documents from the FBI's Secret Wars Against Domestic Dissent.* Boston: South End Press, 1990.

Dodd, Vikram. "Undercover Protester: Fine Line Between Undercover Observer and Agent Provocateur." *The Guardian,* January 11, 2011.

Doward, James and Mark Townsend. "G20 Police 'Used Undercover Men to Incite Crowds.'" *The Guardian,* May 9, 2009.

Flegg, Erin. "Undercover Canada: Police Surveillance of G20 Activists Threatens Future Dissent." *This Magazine* 45, no. 6 (2012).

Hamilton, Johanna, dir. *1971.* Documentary film. New York: Cargo Film and Releasing, 2014. https://www.1971film.com/.

Heid, Bill. "How to Identify an Agent Provocateur." *Off the Grid News.* 2011. https://www.offthegridnews.com/self-defense/how-to-identify-an-agent-provocateur/.

Jany, Libor. "Minneapolis Police Say 'Umbrella Man' Was a White Supremacist Trying to Incite George Floyd Rioting." *Minneapolis Star Tribune,* July 28, 2020. https://www.startribune.com/police-umbrella-man-was-a-white-supremacist-trying-to-incite-floyd-rioting/571932272/.

Kahf, Mohja, and Maciej Bartkowski. "The Syrian Resistance: A Tale of Two Struggles." *OpenDemocracy*, September 23, 2013. https://www.opendemocracy.net/en/civilresistance/syrian-resistance-tale-of-two-struggles/.

Lewis, Paul, and Rob Evans. "Activists Walk Free as Undercover Officer Prompts Collapse of Case." *The Guardian,* January 10, 2011. https://www.theguardian.com/environment/2011/jan/10/activists-undercover-officer-mark-kennedy.

Marx, Gary. "Thoughts on a Neglected Category of Social Movement Participant: The Agent Provocateur and the Informant." *American Journal of Sociology* 80, no. 2 (1974): 402–42.

Mathis, Deborah. "Paradigm Shift: Media Imagery and the BLM Movement." *Minds of the Movement* (blog), July 3, 2020. https://www.nonviolent-conflict.org/blog_post/paradigm-shift-media-imagery-and-the-blm-movement/.

Nepstad, Sharon Erickson. *Nonviolent Revolutions: Civil Resistance in the Late 20th Century.* Oxford: Oxford University Press, 2011.

Russonello, Giovanni. "Fascination and Fear: Covering the Black Panthers." *New York Times*, October 16, 2016.

Sharp, Gene. *Waging Nonviolent Struggle: 20th Century Practice and 21st Century Potential.* Boston: Porter Sargent Publishers, 2005.

Singh, Pashaura. "Deconstructing the Punjab Crisis of 1984: Deer, Hawks, and Siqdārs ('Officials') as Agents of State-Sponsored Violence." *Sikh Formations: Religion, Culture, Theory* 12, nos. 2/3 (2016): 173–90.

Steele, Chris. 2012. "Conversation with Noam Chomsky about Social Justice and the Future." *Jesuit Higher Education* 1, no. 2 (2012): 32–42.

Sterling, Lisha. "Insider Threats: A Closer Look at Infiltrators and Movement Security Culture." *Minds of the Movement* (blog), September 15, 2020. https://www.nonviolent-conflict.org/blog_post/insider-threats-a-closer-look-at-infiltrators-and-movement-security-culture/.

Sweet, Matthew. "Hong Kongers Can't Always Tell Cops from Comrades." *Foreign Policy,* August 20, 2019. https://foreignpolicy.com/2019/08/20/hong-kongers-cant-always-tell-cops-from-comrades/.

Wasow, Omar. "Do Protest Tactics Matter? Evidence from the 1960s Black Insurgency." Unpublished. January 10, 2016. https://www.americanvoiceforfreedom.org/wp-content/uploads/2017/06/Do-Protest-Tactics-Matter-1.pdf.

York, Steve, dir. *A Force More Powerful: A Century of Nonviolent Conflict.* Documentary film. Washington, DC: York-Zimmerman, 2000. https://www.nonviolent-conflict.org/force-powerful-english/.

About the Author

Steve Chase is a longtime organizer, educator, and writer who served as the manager of Academic Initiatives at the International Center on Nonviolent Conflict for four years, during which time he wrote this volume. He is currently the Assistant Director of Solidarity 2020 and Beyond, a solidarity network and community of practice for grassroots movement organizers in the Global South who are learning and applying the skills of advocacy, peacebuilding, and nonviolent resistance to win sustainability, rights, freedom, and justice.

Acknowledgments

The author thanks Hardy Merriman, former President and CEO of the International Center on Nonviolent Conflict (ICNC), for editorial advice and encouraging him to research and write a series of *Minds of the Movement* blogposts that have been used and adapted in this article. The author is also grateful for the editorial feedback on this essay by ICNC colleagues Amber French, Maciej Bartkowski, and Bruce Pearson. Finally, he would like to acknowledge the helpful unpublished research on agent provocateurs developed by Tom Hastings, Associate Professor of Conflict Resolution at Portland State University and Director of the PeaceVoice Program at Oregon Peace Institute. His work alerted the author to some important source material and international examples.